The Inland Seas

The Inland Seas

A JOURNEY THROUGH THE GREAT LAKES

Text by Paul Vasey

Photographs by John de Visser

CHARTWELL
BOOKS, INC.

Published in the United States by
Chartwell Books, Inc.
110 Enterprise Avenue
Secaucus, New Jersey
07094

ISBN: 1-55521-179-8

Design: First Image
Typesetting: Imprint Typesetting
Printed and bound in Hong Kong

Photograph, page 2: A sailboat steers a placid course
near the mouth of the Kaministikwia River.

Contents

Introduction

Once there was a man whose name was Silas John. He was the first serious dreamer I ever met.

He was my father's best and boyhood pal. He was this kind of man: he was tall and thin, and his eyes were large and bright, and his voice was deep and dark, and he was quick to laugh. He loved boats and built many. The largest and last of these was *Persephone*—"like that goddess, she'll live in the sunshine eight months of the year"—and into one of her cabin walls he carved this: "Your dreams are all you own."

One of his dreams ("ever since I was a little knee-higher like you") was to sail through the Great Lakes. And, as he said as he stood in the cockpit and caught my duffel bag, "every captain needs a crew for a trip such as this."

That was thirty years ago.

"In the beginning," said Silas John, "there was the earth and all that was on it, and all that was on it was as verdant as Eden itself. The forests were full of wildlife of every sort and size, and the air alive with the songs and cries of birds of every description and hue. I think that's the thing which would have struck you: the color and the noise.

"Then, no one knows why exactly, the earth's atmosphere began to cool and it started to snow and wouldn't quit. The snows piled and drifted and swept all across the northern half of what we know now as North America, and eventually the snow obliterated every feature of the landscape. In all this vast and featureless desert there wouldn't have been one living soul. All the birds, all the animals, all the fishes and insects, every living creature fled for its life, or lost it. And the thing which would have struck you would have been the silence, an utter chilling silence as would greet you at the end of the earth."

Silas paused and looked up at the jib. "Haul in on that sheet. Just a hair."

The jib quit its riffing. *Persephone* put her shoulder to the waves, and bore down that sun-sparkled day toward the bay's distant, greening hills.

"For thousands of years," said Silas, "it was winter, and the snow which fell never melted. The weight of the snow at the surface compressed the snow at the bottom into ice, and the ice got thicker and thicker. Eventually, all of what we now call Canada—from Vancouver Island to Newfoundland, from the Arctic to the northern part of what is now the United States—all of it was buried beneath a mile or two of ice."

"Silas!"

"Serious. Two miles thick anyway. Here, take the tiller."

The tiller was a dragon whose head— inch-long fangs and bulging eyes—Silas had carved to frighten off any evil spirits which might have wanted to sneak aboard, as evil spirits are known to do now and again, and "as anybody knows," said Silas, "who has read *Moby Dick*."

"Keep her fixed on that headland."

Silas John, tin of tobacco between his knees, commenced the rolling of a smoke—cheating, the two-handed way.

"The weight of all that ice was such that it forced itself into motion: the center forcing the edges outward, like if you pressed putty with the palm of your hand. And that's how the glaciers were born. They moved six, eight, a dozen feet a day, and nothing could stop their advance. They ground the biggest trees into dust, and sheered the tops right off the mountains. The only thing which could have brought them to a halt was warmth, and there wasn't much of that this side of Kansas.

"So the glaciers ground this way and that, retreating and advancing for a million years. Then, who knows why, the earth's atmosphere began warming, and the glaciers began melting, and they melted all the way back to the Arctic, and a new world was revealed.

"Riverbeds had been gouged into valleys, and valleys had become canyons. The water which had been ice flowed into these valleys and canyons, and they became lakes—the largest bodies of fresh water on the face of the earth. And that," said Silas John, "is what we're sailing on."

I was eleven that summer—an age when adventure is not merely possible in the life of a boy, but entirely likely.

"Silas John called last night," said my father. "From Goderich. He says he's in need of crew. I told him I didn't think he had to look any further, but you can tell him yourself. He's to call again tonight, from Southampton."

It was late in June. Since the middle of May we had been receiving these calls, from places whose names I had circled on the map tacked to the wall above my bed: Port Colborne and Port Stanley, Kingsville and Put-In-Bay, Detroit and Port Huron, as Silas John made his meandering way, west by north through the Great Lakes, toward our home in Owen Sound.

It was neither stated nor hinted that I would go with him on his voyage of discovery, but from that moment in January, when he kicked off his boots by our woodstove and spread his charts over our kitchen table, I never doubted this would somehow come to pass. On this, the third day of our voyage, we were nearing the eastern shore of Georgian Bay, a dozen miles or so above the town of Parry Sound.

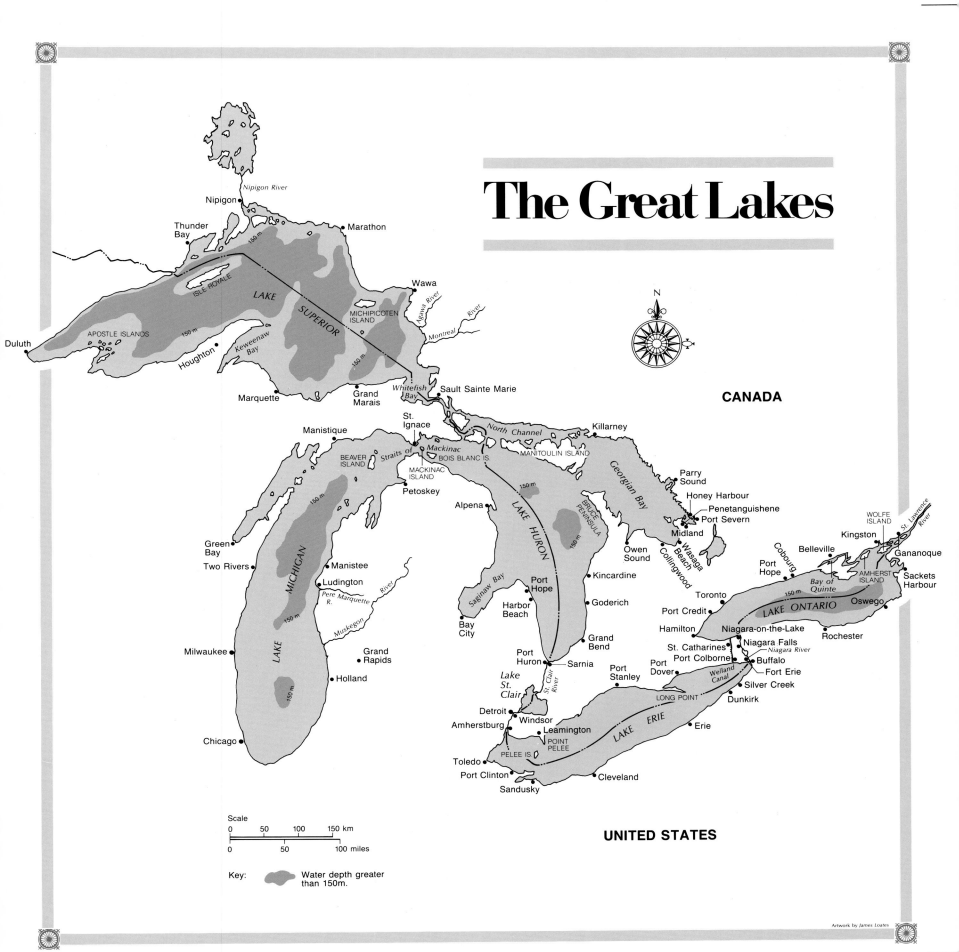

The Great Lakes

Nipigon River

Nipigon

Thunder Bay

Marathon

ISLE ROYALE

LAKE

SUPERIOR

Wawa

Agawa River

MICHIPICOTEN ISLAND

Montreal River

APOSTLE ISLANDS

150 m

Duluth

Keweenaw Bay

Houghton

150 m

Marquette

Grand Marais

Whitefish Bay

Sault Sainte Marie

CANADA

Manistique

St. Ignace

North Channel

Killarney

BEAVER ISLAND

Straits of Mackinac

BOIS BLANC IS.

MANITOULIN ISLAND

MACKINAC ISLAND

Georgian Bay

Parry Sound

Petoskey

Alpena

150 m

BRUCE PENINSULA

Honey Harbour

Penetanguishene

Port Severn

Midland

WOLFE ISLAND

St. Lawrence River

Green Bay

Two Rivers

MICHIGAN

Manistee

Ludington

Pere Marquette R.

LAKE HURON

Owen Sound

Wasaga Beach

Collingwood

Kingston

Cobourg

Belleville

Port Hope

AMHERST ISLAND

Gananoque

Sackets Harbour

River

150 m

Kincardine

Toronto

Bay of Quinte

Port Hope

150 m

Harbor Beach

Goderich

Port Credit

LAKE ONTARIO

150 m

Oswego

Milwaukee

Muskegon River

Saginaw Bay

Grand Rapids

Bay City

Port Hope

Grand Bend

Hamilton

Niagara-on-the-Lake

Rochester

150 m

Holland

Port Huron

Sarnia

St. Catharines

Niagara Falls

Niagara River

Port Stanley

Port Dover

Port Colborne

Buffalo

Fort Erie

Chicago

Lake St. Clair

St. Clair River

LONG POINT

Welland Canal

Silver Creek

Dunkirk

Detroit

Windsor

Leamington

LAKE ERIE

Erie

Amherstburg

POINT PELEE

Toledo

PELEE IS.

Port Clinton

Cleveland

Sandusky

UNITED STATES

Scale

0   50   100   150 km

0   50   100 miles

Key: Water depth greater than 150m.

Artwork by James Loates

7

"That," said Silas, nodding toward an island delineated against the more distant mainland, "is our anchorage. Forward you go. We'll bring in the jib now."

Silas John had been ruined early in life by Conrad and Melville, and the tales and journals of explorers and solo sailors. By the time he turned fourteen, he wanted simply and only to build boats and sail them, to have the heavens above him and the water below him, and the wind forever in his face and in his hair. So, though "he could have been anything," my father said, "a doctor or an architect, anything at all," he worked instead on the night shift in a factory in Toronto, and spent his days doing the only thing that mattered.

The only thing that had mattered, for the better part of the previous four years, was the construction of *Persephone*—a yawl, thirty-six feet long from her bow to her transom—from a great pile of white-oak and teak planks, which had been unceremoniously dumped from a flat-bed truck onto the muddied earth beside Silas' rented, river-facing, grayboard barn, one day in the spring of his forty-first year.

A year and a little from the day of her Credit River launching, *Persephone* lay at anchor in a boulders-rubbled narrows behind a bristle-backed island on Georgian Bay's east coast. In a clearing, in a cove, there was a pine-log cabin, but otherwise no evidence man had ever passed this way. The air was redolent of fir and balsam and pine. The afternoon's silence was startled apart, only occasionally, by the cries of the gulls, and the songs of birds whose names I could not guess. It was toward dusk when the canoe approached.

The man who stepped onto *Persephone*'s teak deck was short and bow-legged, ample of belly and thinning of hair, and wore a beard like General Custer's. He was a painter. He had built the cabin in the cove with his own hands, and he took his living from the lake and the land as much as possible, and he spent his days painting whatever he felt about whatever he saw around him. "It was a little like living in paradise," he said, "or deep in the misted past."

"Once upon a time," he said, "all the shores of all the lakes looked, and smelled and sounded like this. Indians hunted and fished, and in ten thousand years they did not disturb the land, or the cycle of life upon it, as much as the European invaders did in their first hundred. They were no less efficient with an arrow or a spear, but the natives lacked the one characteristic that made such wanton destruction of the land inevitable. Greed relies on a concept of ownership and this the Indians did not understand. The land was no more theirs than the stars. They were passing through this land and life, and made use of what they needed, and left the rest for those who would follow.

"Those who followed had no such respect for the land, or devotion to the gods who inhabited it, and made it abundant. The natives," said the painter, "were living on borrowed time."

"The French happened on North America by accident. They were really looking for Cathay and all its riches in spices and jewels. They figured North America was nothing more than a hurdle, and they did their best to find passage through it or around it, to their intended goal. They kept trying, by various routes, and in 1610 Samuel de Champlain sent young Etienne Brulé by another—the Ottawa River—to see what he could find. What he found, crossing Lake Nipissing and descending the French River, was Georgian Bay.

"Five years later he would discover the second of the Great Lakes, which the Indians called "Ontario," which meant "sparkling waters." Two years after that, returning to Lake Huron, he would coast the north shore all the way to the Sault— the mile-long rapids which missionaries would christen Sainte Marie, and beyond which lay the greatest lake of all.

"But Cathay remained as unreachable as ever, and the thriving fur trade was nothing more than a consolation prize.

"Champlain, in the year before he died, attempted once more to find this route to the east, sending Jean Nicolet in search of a lake said to lie beyond Huron. Nicolet paddled west, through the Straits of Mackinac, and found the lake the Indians called Mitchiganous. So certain was he that he would find Cathay, that Nicolet brought along a robe of embroidered silk elaborate enough to impress the Emperor of China. He was wearing it when he stepped onto the shores of Green Bay and met the local residents, the Winnebagos.

"More than three decades would pass before the first Frenchman stood on the shores of Lake Erie. In order to reach it, explorers had to cross Lake Ontario, which was in the heart of land controlled by the Iroquois. The Iroquois were no great fans of the French—Champlain had befriended their neighbors and enemies, the Hurons—and it wasn't until 1669 that a peace of sorts was declared, and the country safe enough to travel, and it was in that year that Louis Jolliet got his first look at Erie.

"So the Europeans had finally discovered all the Great Lakes. Having discovered them, they laid claim to all that was in and around them. The mystified Hurons and Chippewas, Iroquois and Sioux, were in more trouble than they could have imagined."

We made tea for the painter, and sat in the cockpit for a long while that night, and he and Silas John talked of many things: of the crossing and divergence of the paths of their lives; of the painter's voyage in the woods; and Silas John's on the lakes; and of the nature of the things which lured them each along.

Late in the night as he rose to go, the painter said, "So long as you know you're searching for something, you'll eventually find it. Even if you don't know precisely what it is. Just like the explorers."

He turned to me. "You don't know what we're talking about, do you?

"You will," said the painter. "Some day you will."

Opposite page: A youth watches the waves roll in, on a beach on Lake Erie.

Lake Superior

Of all the Great Lakes, Superior is the most imposing: three hundred and fifty miles from Duluth in the west, to the rapids of Sainte Marie in the east; one hundred and sixty from the barrel-chested north shore to the ore-treasured south; 1,300 feet deep at her center.

Her name is synonymous with northern beauty. Sheer granite bluffs plunge a thousand feet or more into the gray-green combers; sweeping, pink-pebbled beaches end abruptly at headlands spiked with pines; frenzied, gorge-running rivers plume their way to the inland sea.

Her moods are no less impressive. Her lightless depths are littered with the boats and the bones of those luckless or foolish enough to be caught along a shelterless stretch of her coast in a storm.

Odd, then, it is not such facts or impressions that linger most in memory, but rather the tales Silas told, as we coasted Superior's daunting shores. Many of these stories touched upon the lives and the gods of the people who had lived around Superior for 10,000 years before the Europeans arrived.

The first people to make the country around Lake Superior their home led intensely spiritual lives. The spirits of the dead—the ever-present mystery of the northern lights—danced over their heads. Their gods were all around them. They orchestrated the rising of the sun and the waning of the moon. When in a felicitous mood, they caused plants and crops to grow, and animals and fish to multiply abundantly. When angered or offended, they caused the rivers and the lake to rage, and the earth to become barren.

The natives did not dare take more from the lake or the woods than they required for their food, their clothing, or their shelter. It was with reverence and awe and gratitude—offering prayers of thanks to their victims—they took even this.

"A lot of silly superstition," said Silas John, "at least as far as the missionaries were concerned. They did their best to convince the Indians to disavow their gods. Too bad," said Silas, "that they were so successful, because the gods of the Indians protected this country more effectively than the gods of trade and commerce could." He went on at some length about the sacred being profaned, and only once again that summer—in the pollution-plumed Chemical Valley at the mouth of the St. Clair River—would I see him approach anger.

What had got him going were the paintings on the rocks of Agawa.

There are hundreds of these centuries-old paintings—child-like in their simplicity, chilling in their antiquity—all through the north country. How these pictures, depicting the natives' gods, travels, triumphs and disasters, have survived generation upon generation of ice, and rain, and heat is anyone's guess. But survive they do, and they tell us much about the natives' way of life.

"That one," said Silas, "is thought to be a god called Mishipizhiw. If the lake was thrashing or a river running dangerously fast, swamping canoes and drowning people, you could lay money on him being behind it."

I made a picture of another of these gods—four-legged, ferociously-tailed—in my scribbler/journal and beneath it wrote, "Maymaygwayshi, god of the rocks. Silas says he lives inside the rocks, especially rocks with cracks and caves. Indians say they have seen him paddling a canoe up to a rock face and disappearing right into it. He steals fish from the nets when no one is looking. Silas says Indians leave tobacco on rock ledges to buy him off."

"Do you believe all that stuff?"

"Let's put it this way," said Silas. "The older I get, the less inclined I am to be a doubter."

The gods of the Indians were all but doomed from the dawning of the day when Claude Allouez, priest of the god of the Europeans, pushed his canoe away from the shores of Bawating, and ghosted up the St. Mary's River and out onto the great, gray lake itself. Allouez, in that fall of 1665, would go on to coast the lake, and draw a map of what he saw, and reopen a mission—La Pointe du St. Esprit—near the Keweenaw Peninsula on Superior's southern shore.

With his mission and his maps, Allouez unlocked the lake and through this open gate, in earnest, came the voyageurs and traders—first French, later English—in search of their fortune in furs.

These voyageurs were unbelievably hardy. They could paddle forty or fifty strokes a minute, for a dozen or more hours a day. They often averaged sixty to eighty miles between breakfast and dusk. In their canoes, some of which were nearly forty feet long, they could carry as much as three tons of trade goods or furs. On portage, they commonly shouldered packs weighing 180 pounds and would jog this burden half a mile up the trail. "Funny thing," said Silas, "most of them couldn't swim a stroke."

So relentless were the trappers and traders that within 200 years of Allouez's coasting of the lake its shore had already become eerily silent. The traders were forced to move west, via the Grand Portage, in search of the pelts of the beaver and fox, the wolf and the bear.

But no vacuum remains for long, and into the vacuum left by the end of the fur trade came fortune hunters of another stripe. As far back as Allouez's time, the newcomers had heard of troves of treasured minerals and metals. The four-ton copper boulder in the Ontonagon River was merely a symbol of the wealth which was surely theirs for the finding.

Find it they did, and the word spread, and the copper rush of the mid-nineteenth century had all the trappings of the gold rush in the north. Prospectors swarmed in, campsites and shanty towns appeared all along the south shore, and during the last half of the century nearly half of all the copper mined in the United States came from that region. One mine alone turned a profit of $20,000 a month.

One thing leads to another. When the copper prospectors found their compasses going wild, they looked down at the ground and found something just as valuable. And the rush for iron ore was on.

"Here's a story for you," said Silas, "and a true one. There were once seven brothers. Merritt was their name, and their old dad used to point to the west and say, there's ore out there, mark my word. It had already been found to the east and the south.

"Well, look the boys did, for the next twenty years. One of them, Cassius was his name, landed a job with a crew mapping a route for a rail line, which would go from Duluth to Winnipeg. And one day he kicked a chunk of rock, right there in the heart of the country his dad had told them so long ago to scour.

"The next year Cassius and all his brothers came back to that area, with a season's worth of equipment and supplies. What they found was the Mesabi Range, the largest of the five ranges which ring Superior.

"It was the ore," Silas said, "that really altered Superior's fate, for good or ill, once and for all. It was the need to get the ore out that led to the building of canals and locks to bypass the rapids at Sainte Marie.

"Once passage was made easy, all kinds of trade and commerce and industry were possible. The old towns—Duluth and Sault Sainte Marie—grew and new ones—Wawa, Marquette, Houghton, Nipigon, Schreiber—sprouted and took root.

"Superior belonged to the invaders."

Tugboats go about their business near Thunder Bay.

Opposite page: The Trans-Canada Highway appears to emerge from Lake Superior, at Rossport, Ontario.

Following pages: The water runs fast at the shallow mouth of the Sand River.

Rough northern vegetation edges the shore at Nipigon Bay.

Opposite page: A wooden trestle bridge partly screens the town of Marquette, Michigan.

Water has worn away the shoreline in Pictured
Rocks National Lakeshore, Michigan.

Opposite page: Moss clings to rock on the north
shore.

A sheer cliff rises from the lake at Agawa Bay.

The bluffs near Agawa are famous for the ancient petroglyphs, or inscriptions, painted by Indians.

Following pages: The evening sky is full of threats and portents, over Pancake Bay.

A birch forest has been stripped of its leaves by autumn winds, near Munising, Michigan.

Opposite page: Stones, worn smooth by friction and the action of the water, are banked on the edges of the Montreal River.

Ships like this make up the constant industrial
traffic on the Great Lakes.

The grain elevators and docks hide the lake from residents of Thunder Bay.

Following pages: The storms on Lake Superior can be sudden and deadly. This is merely a squall, at the harbor entrance, Duluth, Minnesota.

Water warmed by the sun gives rise to a morning mist on Lake Superior.

Opposite page: Sibley Provincial Park, near Thunder Bay, is one of the many conservation areas that border the Great Lakes.

Dawn breaks over Old Woman Bay.

A fishing boat is tied to a wooden pier, near Marathon.

Following pages: Nipigon is one of the most picturesque towns on the north shore of Superior.

The Canadian Pacific Railway line curves gently though the bush, on the north shore.

Opposite page: Blueberry shrubs blossom on the rocks beside Lake Superior.

The lake is in a quiet mood, near the mouth of the Montreal River.

Opposite page: The many lakes and rivers surrounding Lake Superior provide excellent sport fishing.

Glacial action smoothed and deposited boulders, like this one beside Lake Superior, as if they were soft pebbles.

Opposite page: The paintings on the rocks, called petroglyphs, suggest the monsters and gods of Indian legends.

Lake Michigan

You cannot be much further removed from the loons-and-geese echoing coasts of Superior than the southern end of Lake Michigan. From Chicago in the west to Michigan City in the east, this once-duned shore seems nothing so much as a sprawl of industry, the sky above it a bruise.

We put in at Chicago only briefly—in need of fuel and fresh water, ice and ice cream—and of that city I recall a sense of being completely overwhelmed. All through that night, sirens echoed in the glass-walled, canyoned streets beyond us, "like the wailing of the damned," and neither of us slept very much, or very well. Silas didn't help matters by his choice of bed-time stories.

He spent much of the evening telling stories about Al Capone, and machine-gunnings, speakeasies and painted ladies, and bodies being chained ankle and wrist and dumped into the river, "probably quite a few from this very wharf."

And he went on in some detail about the sinking of the *Eastland*. "She was a three-decker, a passenger ship. There were dozens of them once, all around the lakes. Long gone now. The only ones I know of, even remotely like them, run from Detroit to an amusement park downriver. You'll see them when we go that way. Anyway, these ships used to take people on cruises all through the lakes, and a company had hired the *Eastland* to take its employees, about two thousand of them, on a cruise for the day.

"They started coming aboard about seven in the morning and, as passengers will, they stood by the rail on the dock side. Pretty soon the ship started to list that way, and the crew opened the cocks to even her off, and then she began listing the other way. The next thing you know, between panicking passengers and water sloshing around in the bilges, the old ship lost her balance and turned over like a steel whale and sank in the river. More than eight hundred drowned."

"Then," said Silas, "there was the time the whole city burned down, right to the ground. Eighteen seventy something. Eighteen thousand buildings destroyed over an area of three square miles. The heat was so intense, even some ships anchored in the river caught fire."

But a city, like a prairie, will grow again from its charcoaled stubble. Chicago rose from its ashes to become one of the Great Lakes' great cities. Her growth was due, in part, to the shipping canal which links her with the riverways which lead all the way to the Gulf of Mexico—"just as Nicolet had a hunch they would"—and opened her to the commerce not only of the lakes, but also of ports around the world.

By the time her streets were teeming with workers shop-and office-bound, we were standing half a mile out and eastward bound.

Someone has described Chicago as a city of big shoulders. Close in, and farther out, it feels and looks exactly like that.

"Say what you will about their missionary zeal, you've got to admit those Jesuits were remarkable men."

Silas was thinking about Jacques Marquette who set out in the spring of 1673 with Louis Jolliet, five voyageurs, some ground corn and a vague notion that beyond the rim of Lake Michigan there lay a river, which would take them all the way to the sea.

Two months later, they had paddled and portaged all the way down the Mississippi to the mouth of the Arkansas River, below where the city of Memphis now stands, and by that fall they were back on Lake Michigan again.

"No mean feat," Silas said, "when you think what it involves: fourteen or sixteen hours a day paddling; all but freezing when you set out, and boiling when you return; sleeping on a bed of branches on some muddy riverbank, with your head in a cloud of mosquitoes."

It was to be the death of Marquette. Though he lived another year and a half, the exhaustion and illness which would claim his life took root on that trip, which took him a thousand miles into the heart of America.

In the spring of 1675, too ill and weak to continue his missionary work among the Illinois Indians, he and some companions set out for "home"—the mission

Marquette had founded at St. Ignace on the Straits of Mackinac. "You can imagine what it must have been like: him so sick and the cold and the rain and the storms of spring. It was a wonder they got as far as they did." They got half way up Lake Michigan's eastern shore.

Marquette told his companions to put ashore at the mouth of a river which had caught his eye and his fancy. They argued for going on, but he refused and they went ashore. He had picked the place he wanted to die. It is called, now, Pere Marquette River. When his friends had got him out of the canoe and more or less comfortable, he told them exactly how he wanted to be buried, "right down to the way he wanted his hands placed on his chest, and what kind of service they were to have." They buried him there, just as he wanted, and if you pass that way you will see the cross on top of the hill near the town of Ludington, which marks the spot.

"Can't imagine what got me in the mood for all this death and dying," said Silas, "but here's another story."

This one ended pretty well straight across the lake from Ludington, but it started one hundred and fifty miles north, near the town of Manistique.

"A sailor named Scheunemanns used to go from Chicago to the north shore every November. He and his crew would cut pine trees, which they took back to Chicago and sold from the deck, seventy-five cents or a dollar apiece, and that money would pretty well keep him through the winter.

"This one year, 1912, they set out for Chicago, their ship loaded with Christmas trees, and found themselves in a bitter blizzard, one of those famous November gales, and the ship was never seen again.

"About a month after it left Manistique, a bottle washed up on the Wisconsin shore and there was a note in it. The note said, 'I guess we are all through.' It went on to say that two of the seventeen crew members had been washed overboard, and that the waves were coming right over the decks. 'God help us,' said the note.

"Fifteen years later, just south of Two Rivers Point, another bottle was found with another note inside. It gave the ship's location, twenty miles south of Two Rivers Point and twenty miles offshore. 'All hands lashed to one line,' the note said. 'Good-bye.'"

North and west of the little tourist town of Charlevoix, which is in the heart of Michigan's most beautiful country, there is an island which, as far as Silas knew, was the site of the only kingdom in all the Great Lakes country.

A century ago, a community of Mormons left southern Wisconsin and followed their self-proclaimed king all the way to Beaver Island. "His reign," said Silas, "came to kind of an unhappy end."

The newcomers were not exactly welcomed with open arms. "But you have to understand," said Silas, "that most men are huddlers. They like to live in close quarters, physically, and intellectually, and spiritually. And they regard those who choose to live apart with a mixture of distrust and suspicion, if not outright hostility.

"Well, these Mormons had probably not cleared their first patch of ground before the mainlanders got to talking about them, and the more they talked, the wilder the stories became. Before very long, the Mormons were thieves, they were pirates, they stole each other's wives and murdered passersby. Just about anything that was impossible to believe, the mainlanders believed about the Mormons.

"They finally worked themselves into such a lather that they convinced the U.S. Army to move in and clear the Mormons right off the island, if not the face of the earth. But before the Army could do anything, the Mormons had a big fight amongst themselves, and the next thing you know, five or six of them have been shot to death and the rest have fled.

"Which is pretty much the same as always happens," Silas figured, "when you try to create a kingdom of heaven here on earth."

A mountain of salt is protected from the elements in Milwaukee.

Opposite page: A beer storage facility at dockside in Manitowoc, Wisconsin.

The early history of the Great Lakes was made by Indians, priests, and soldiers. This statue stands before the Brown County Building, in Green Bay, Wisconsin.

Lighthouses, like this one in Milwaukee harbor, may still be useful as landmarks to sailors despite the development of other aids to navigation.

The "Windy City," Chicago, rises impressively
from Lake Michigan.

The tower in the foreground was the only building to survive the fire which razed Chicago in the 1870s.

Following pages: After a storm, the sun breaks through black clouds, at Ludington, a resort town in Michigan.

Each figure represents a lake in the Fountain of the Great Lakes outside the Chicago Art Institute.

An icy stillness settles over Traverse City.

Following pages: The still waters reflect the warehouses and church of Two Rivers, Wisconsin.

Lakefront homes in Petoskey, Michigan: some
are closed for the winter; others lived in
year-round.

Opposite page: A number of lighthouses are
preserved as museums. This one is in Michigan
City.

The simple structure of the bridge in Milwaukee Harbor gives it an abstract quality.

Preceding pages: The fishing industry continues to be important in towns like Port Washington, Wisconsin.

Opposite page: A bicycle rack is there for the convenience of bathers at the beach in Holland, Michigan.

After the summer season, a pleasure craft in
Holland, Michigan, is hauled ashore for
maintenance.

Preceding pages: Stark, autumnal trees frame a
lighthouse in Holland, Michigan.

A dockside dumping ground in Two Rivers holds nautical treasures and old-fashioned trash.

Lake Huron

At the corner of Lakes Michigan and Huron, there are a pair of old forts, one on the mainland and one on an island, and concerning these forts Silas had a tale apiece.

"That one," he said, nodding in the direction of the fort in the shadows of the Mackinac Bridge, "was built by the French in the eighteenth century for an obvious reason: from it, they could control the traffic through the Straits.

"Well you know how wars are: you win some and you lose some. When the French lost the Plains of Abraham, they lost Michilimackinac as well, and a year or so later, in their bright red uniforms and proud as punch, the British marched up and claimed their prize.

"The Indians were not impressed. They found the British stuffy, formal and overweening but, more serious than that, felt they stood to lose a lot more land under the British than they had under the French.

"The upshot was that Chief Pontiac spent the winter of 1762 convincing tribes all across the northwest to make one last stand against the British the following summer.

"The day they picked was the King's birthday.

"That day the Indians were playing lacrosse in the field near the fort, and one fellow fired the ball over the stockade. He then went up and knocked on the gate and said, 'mind if I get my ball?'

"The officer who answered the knock had either never heard the story about the Trojan Horse, or he'd raised one too many glasses of grog in honor of old George the Third, or both.

"As soon as he opened the gate, the knives were out. Within a matter of minutes, 71 British soldiers were either scalped or tomahawked to death.

"The British," said Silas, "were slow learners." It took them another twenty years to figure that Mackinac Island might be a safer place to have a fort.

"Nice fort," said Silas, motioning toward the one on the hill on Mackinac Island. "The British liked it and they didn't like it one bit when they lost it, by treaty, after the revolutionary war. Took it back, first chance they had, which was the War of 1812, and promptly lost it again, and for good, in the treaty which carved things up after that war."

She might have been one of those ghost ships that, having foundered and failed in its contest of wills with the inland seas, is doomed to sail now and ever, with never a prayer of putting in once more at the flags-flying, wives-waving port called home.

She rose from the mists of the morning, this red-sailed schooner, like a multi-winged moth to the pale and rising sun. She must have been more than one hundred feet long, and carried a dozen flaming sails from her triple masts. "I've never seen so much canvas over one deck," said Silas.

We were bound east, she west, and though in no fairer patch of wind, she seemed to move as though under power. She glided past us, no more than a quarter mile distant, and the morning pulled its shroud around her.

"You'll not see the likes of her again soon," said Silas, "though once you'd never have given her more than a second glance."

Once, and not that long ago, such ships, many larger, most her size or a little smaller, were as unremarkable as the tugs and freighters which ply the lakes today.

"At the peak and prime of their time," said Silas, "there were two thousand sailing ships working the Great Lakes. They carried ore from the ranges of Superior to the steel mills on the southern coasts of Lake Michigan and Lake Erie.

They carried manufactured goods from the cities of the south on their upward voyages. They were the lifeblood of the towns which materialized around the shores of the lakes. Some of the best of these ships were built and launched here, in the north, and they sailed, some of them, for more than half a century."

You need only have listened to Silas John on the subject of sailing ships to realize he was born a century too late. "It is a wise man," he said, "who lives his life attuned to the rhythms of nature. You tell me how you can hear the rhythms of nature, or anything else, above the throbbing of an engine.

"The only thing you can hear above that racket is the call of profit. To men who answer such a call, the sound of the wind in the rigging, and the lazy slapping of water against a wooden hull, well, that's just the sound of coins slipping through their fingers."

The first of the steamers sailed out onto the lakes in 1816. They were harbingers, Silas said, of the day when the last of these graceful sailing ships would be stripped of her deckhouses and spars, and converted into a barge to be towed by some foul-smelling, soot-spewing, merchant's excuse for a boat.

"It would be better to sink in a storm than to die a death such as that."

"Life," Silas said, "sometimes gives us people to show us the error of our ways. And sometimes it gives us people to confirm, by the mirror reflection of our dreams and desires, the rightness of the leanings of our hearts."

It was for this latter reason, apparently, that Life gave us the silver-haired man in the forty-four-foot Chris Craft cruiser.

We had run from squally weather into one of those inlets for which Lake Huron's North Channel is fabled. The inlet narrowed, half a mile from open water, to no more than twenty feet, a neck bordered on either side by perpendicular faces of moss-bearded granite. Beyond this gate lay one of the north shore's true treasures: a lagoon a quarter mile across, its unrippled face black with the reflections of the pines which browed the bluffs which enclosed it.

On the far side—"how'd he get that thing in here?"—was the cruiser, moored by lines slung around the trunks of those dwarf trees that manage, somehow, to grow right out of the rock itself.

If Silas wasn't thinking, right that moment, of circling the lagoon and leaving, I'd have eaten the anchor I was holding.

Silas John had a loathing of motor boats quite beyond belief and bounds. If one were to shoal up and begin to sink before him, it would be a coin toss whether he would go to the aid of its crew. In most circumstances he refused to acknowledge their existence.

"It's bottomless," said the silver-haired man. "Anchor's no good. You'll have to tie up."

What made Silas decide to do so, I'll never guess, but tie up we did a couple of dozen yards ahead of the cruiser. No sooner had we made fast than a launch pulled alongside, and there he was: white-haired chest, tattered jeans, disintegrating deck shoes and a smile this wide. "We're just observing the cocktail hour. I trust you'll join us."

Silas smiled one of his "how do we get out of this?" smiles and so it was we wound up, late in the night, sitting on deck chairs, watching the moonlight, Silas talking, Edgar talking, Silas and Edgar singing campfire songs while Edgar picked out the tune on his ancient mandolin.

Edgar was from Detroit. He had owned a tool-and-die shop and made a lot of money, and he made a lot more when he sold the place. "The doctor finished up the examination and he looked at me and said 'Ed,' he said, 'you're a dead man.' Gave me six months, eight or nine tops. So what's a guy to do? I sold the shop, and

sold the house, and sold the car and I went out and bought this boat." And off he went, stocked to the gunwales with bourbon and steaks, to spend the rest of his life on the lakes he had loved since he was a kid my age.

"The doctor was either wrong or the best friend I ever had." Because, for the last four years, Edgar had been cruising the lakes in summer, and the Gulf in winter, and he'd never been happier.

Waving good-bye the following morning, Silas grinned at me and said: "Goes to show you should never judge a book by a cover, or a man by his boat."

You've never seen a storm until—out of sight of land—you've seen one from the deck of a boat.

This one had caught us more or less by surprise, though as Silas said at least twice, "it's my own damned fault."

Storms aren't supposed to come in pairs. We had been laid up two days in Killarney, which is no hardship at all, waiting for one to blow over. Despite the color of the sunset on the second night, and the ambivalent complexion of the next morning's sky, we shipped our lines just past dawn for our trip across the gap between Manitoulin Island and the tip of the Bruce Peninsula.

The lake was still upset, one wash coming west from Georgian Bay, and another east from the lake itself, and the wind was just as confused. It had been behind us and then athwart us from the east, and in the space of twenty minutes switched around and stiffened out of the north northwest, and freshened until it was blowing the foam off the waves.

It was about then Silas sent me below for our life preservers, and the safety lines which snap onto the lifelines which run around the deck. "So if you're washed over you'll first of all float and secondly can hand-over-hand yourself back aboard." His laugh and smile did little to undo the knot in my stomach.

"Here, you take her."

As I guided her down one wave and up the next, Silas reefed in the main until,

rolled around the boom, it presented no more than half its full face into the wind. If it weren't for the waves, which we were starting to take blue over the bow, we'd have hauled in the jib and put up a smaller one, but there was time now only for sliding in the gangway shutters and closing the hatch.

"I think we're in for a ride."

A ride is not quite adequate to describe the trip we had, nor are any other words sufficient to convey the power and frightening beauty of the lake as we pitched and wallowed our way south.

I would have been sick if I hadn't been so frightened, "and I would've been scared stripeless if I hadn't been so damned busy," said Silas. And never were two slickered and soaked sailors happier than when, an eternity later, we ducked into the lee of one of the islands which crown the tip of the Bruce.

"That," said Silas, "was a small taste of what the lakes can offer, and by the standards of a full-fledged November gale, it wasn't much more than a stiff breeze."

These "widow-makers," as Silas called them, are legendary. That night, as "a fitting bedtime tale," he told me of the worst storm ever to hit the lakes while the rigging sang with the dying breath of our day's blow.

That storm of 1913 lasted five days. For one sixteen-hour stretch, the winds were never under 60 miles an hour. The waves were 35 to 40 feet, and some of them, "the freak ones which break a freighter's back and drive her to the bottom," were probably twice that. "And if you've ever wondered what it means to say 'the wrath of God,' that gives you some idea."

By the time that great storm finally died, at least ten ships had gone down, eight of them with all hands. At least twenty more were driven up on one shoal or shore or another, and in all, 248 men either drowned or froze to death.

"Something to think about," said Silas, pouring himself another finger of whiskey, "when you're saying your prayers."

Huckleberry Finn—or, at least, his modern counterpart—displays his catch at lakeside in Goderich.

Opposite page: A sailboat approaches a lighthouse in Kincardine, Ontario.

Following pages: Ice lines the entrance to Lake St. Clair, at Sarnia.

Ships wait to enter the St. Clair River after an
accident has blocked the passage.

Huts give shelter to ice-fishermen on Georgian Bay, near Penetang.

The International Bridge, over the St. Clair
River, links Port Huron and Sarnia.

Erosion has sculpted the stone into strange shapes on Flowerpot Island, near Tobermory.

A public beach can be a private place.

Opposite page: Georgian Bay, famous for shipwrecks, is also a major resort area.

Following pages: The petrochemical plants in Sarnia make lurid colors in the night sky.

A freighter in the St. Clair River: the Great
Lakes link the continent's heartland to the
markets of the world.

The shipping season ends when the St. Lawrence River freezes up. This ship in Sarnia is wintering in dry dock.

The Canadian Pacific Railway Station in
Goderich, Ontario, has been maintained despite
the decline in passenger traffic.

Straits of Mackinac: the photograph was taken
with a long exposure to reveal the motion of the
bridge in a gale-force wind.

Following pages: An autumn storm sends spray
skyward at Grand Bend.

Will the table tip? A man contemplates the water at Wasaga Beach.

Opposite page: Children playing on the beach by Georgian Bay.

Lake Erie

"Hard to picture it now," Silas said, as we rode the currents of the Detroit River, "but three hundred years ago La Salle figured this was about as close to Eden as he was going to get."

When he passed this way on the *Griffon*'s maiden voyage, La Salle wrote in his journals of the wildlife he saw—deer and bears—and the broad open plains bordered by walnut and chestnut trees, and natural orchards of plum and apple. "He even found some wild grapes which made a passable wine."

Twenty years later Cadillac, the self-made nobleman, established an outpost on the north shore which eventually grew, thanks to Henry Ford, to become the automotive capital of the United States, and one of the largest cities on the Great Lakes. The little town of Sandwich, which the French fort spawned across the river, site of the oldest continuous settlement in Ontario, was long ago swallowed up by Windsor.

The mile-wide river between them has become one of the busiest thoroughfares in North America. "A pretty exciting place, half a century ago. Folks used to come down to the riverbanks after dusk to watch the gunfire up and down the river," as rum-runners did their best to outsmart the police, who tried vainly to stem the flow of liquor from the Canadian shore to the American.

Both countries had outlawed the sale and consumption of liquor in public places, and the U.S. also forbade its manufacture. "But in Canada, they could make the stuff and sell it, so long as it was shipped to a country where prohibition was not in force. No problem. Where the government export permit said 'destination,' the rum-runners just wrote in, 'Cuba.' Then they pulled up to the distillery docks in their rowboats and runabouts, handed in their permits, loaded up and took off. An hour later they'd be back for another load. Some guys made six trips to Cuba in one day."

We passed under the Ambassador Bridge, the longest international suspension span in the world. We skirted the foul-breathed behemoth squatting on Zug Island (of which Silas said, "never was an island ever more appropriately named") and we came to Amherstburg which, a century and a half ago, was known as Fort Malden, a bustling military stronghold.

The Americans had lost more battles and skirmishes than they wanted to count in the early stages of the War of 1812. Resolved to win at least one, they set about building a fleet of ships down the lake, at Erie.

The British were building one of their own in the Navy Yard at Malden, but they didn't have time to put all the finishing touches on the *Detroit* before they heard, in September of 1813, that Oliver Perry had finished his ships, and was sailing down the lake.

So the almost-finished *Detroit* was pushed down the ways and Robert Barclay set off, with five other ships, to meet his foe.

We followed Barclay's route the thirty miles south and east to Put-In-Bay where, early one morning, Perry was awakened by a crew member calling from the crow's nest that the horizon was covered with sail.

"War," said Silas, "is a strange and savage spectacle, and never more so than when it is conducted in slow motion, with an air of civility." And this was never more evident than in the only battle fought on the Great Lakes.

It was a nearly windless day. The American squadron drifted for more than an hour before coming within range of the British, whose flagship promptly battered Perry's *Lawrence* to pieces. Perry had to take a skiff to her sister ship, the *Niagara*, and conduct the rest of the battle from her decks.

This "great cumbersome dance of death" went on for four hours, with the ships positioning and repositioning themselves as best they could. Finally, with tattered sails and scarcely a breath of wind, Perry managed to break the British line, open fire on both sides and save the American day. No sooner had the smoke settled than he sat down and wrote to his superiors: "We have met the enemy and they are ours."

It was a costly victory: twenty-seven of Perry's men died and ninety-six were wounded; forty-one British sailors were killed, ninety-four wounded.

"When it was over, Perry returned to the decks of the *Lawrence* and waited for the British officers to arrive. It was all very genteel. The British officers removed their swords and offered them to Perry, hilt-first. Perry, ever the young gentleman, politely declined. Then they all returned to their ships and sailed to Put-In-Bay where Perry, with his arm around Barclay's shoulders, marched to the graveyard where they buried their dead. Barclay later wrote home to say what a terrific fellow this Perry was." Silas smiled. "You figure it out. I can't."

Going north from Put-In-Bay toward Pelee Island, you pass a little island which very nearly straddles the international line and which is named, aptly, Middle Island.

"It's Canada's southernmost piece of land and should be," Silas said, "a national park or preserve, but the American who owns it has no intention of selling it."

On the way up the lakes Silas had met an old fisherman who once survived a three-day December blow on Middle Island. He'd set out to haul nets, and he wasn't half done clearing the first of them, when the storm broke. He managed to work his way into the lee of the island, beach his boat, and secure it by a line to a tree. He took refuge in the lone, abandoned house and, with a fire and some frozen fish, managed to live "quite king-like" until the storm broke. He made it home to the mainland on the fourth day, just in time for his own wake which quickly turned, he said, "into a most wonderful party."

As the old man said, Lake Erie "has a perfect quick temper." Sunday sailors and the crews of Erie's unique, turtle-back fishing tugs know this only too well.

By no means a small lake—at 241 miles it is 35 longer than Huron—it is by far the most shallow. Superior is more than 1,300 feet in her center, Michigan 925, Ontario 804 and Huron 750, but Erie, at her deepest, is only 210 and her coastal waters, laced with reefs and shoals, are more shallow still.

A stiff blow out of either the east or west creates formidable waves at the opposite end, and the water tends to "pile up." In one savage storm early this century, the water level at Buffalo rose 20 feet. Ships were ripped from their moorings and floated in the streets. Houses were washed away and their occupants drowned.

Erie's winds are famously fickle. "They'll switch from west to east in a matter of minutes. Many's the sailor who, smug and settled in the lee of Point Pelee or Long Point, suddenly finds himself being pounded ashore."

There is a chart of Long Point upon which a man has marked with an X the locations where ships have gone down. They number more than one hundred.

"Down around Port Stanley, Port Rowan—Port Rowan I think it was," said Silas, "a ship was driven upon the shoals this one time, and began to break up. Her cargo, all packed in crates, started to wash away. Unluckily for the crew, the cargo was whiskey. While they hollered for someone to work them out a line so they could get safely ashore, men and women and children were busy carting off the cargo. The whole town, they say, was drunk for days.

"All in all," Silas said, "you see a storm coming and you'd best head for any harbor you can find."

The north and south shores of Lake Erie are a study in contrasts. There are probably more people living in and around Cleveland than live in all the north-shore towns and villages combined.

While the American shore is heavily industrialized and densely populated, the economy of the north rests primarily on the fortunes of farmers and fishermen.

It was the building of the Erie Canal, really, that made the difference. Before the canal was completed in 1825, the whole Lake Erie territory was frontier. When Buffalo was linked to the Hudson River and, by the Hudson, to the Atlantic, that changed overnight. Where once it took a week or more to get goods from New York by cart or wagon, it now took only a few days, and the cost of shipping goods dropped ninety per cent.

These towns had long had access to the riches of the north, but they now had an easy route to the markets of the east as well. "It was," said Silas, "a match made in industrial heaven."

And it transformed places like Buffalo from sleepy towns—"forty to fifty houses a decade before the canal opened"—into ports which thrived on the shipment of grain and minerals and lumber from the west, and manufactured goods from the east.

When Canada opened the Welland Canal four years later, "the upper lakes were truly open for business."

It was in the first of Welland's locks, wedged kitty-corner an arm's length from the towering bow of an 800-foot freighter—"gives a new meaning to the word 'intimidation' doesn't it?"—that we began our 326-foot descent to the last of our lakes.

Cranes stand ready to unload a freighter in Cleveland, Ohio.

Opposite page: The Windsor–Detroit rail ferry links two cities dependent on the auto industry.

Following pages: Detroit—"Motor City"—seen from the Canadian side, at Windsor.

Buffalo at work: the sky at sunrise is aglow in the
chilly air.

The grain elevators in Buffalo, New York: a ship pulls in.

Perry's flagship, *Niagara*, has been preserved in Erie, Pennsylvania.

Opposite page: The flag is reflected in a window on the town square, Silver Creek, New York.

The sun sets over Lake Erie, near Buffalo.

Industries, old and new, continue cheek-by-jowl in Ashtabula, Ohio.

Following pages: The Peace Bridge links Canada and the United States at Fort Erie.

Trucks back up and are tipped to unload grain into grain elevators in Toledo, Ohio.

The sun shines on downtown Buffalo.

Cleveland, Ohio, is situated on one of the more densely-populated shorelines on the Great Lakes.

The monument honors Cleveland's war dead.

A forest of masts screens the view of a Buffalo
marina.

You can't miss the sign, at least, in Port Clinton, Ohio.

Opposite page: The Canadawa Creek provides placid shelter from the lake, near Dunkirk, New York.

Student soldiers prime the cannon at Old Fort
Erie.

The Ambassador Bridge joins Windsor, Canada and Detroit, U.S.A.

Following pages: The lake is picturesquely frozen over at Port Stanley.

A pause for reflection at the Genesee County
Pioneer Village, near Rochester, New York.

Fishing nets are hung out to dry in Port Dover, Ontario.

The Niagara wine-growing industry gains credibility year-by-year: vineyards on the banks of Lake Erie.

Opposite page: The Point Pelee Bird Sanctuary is one of the better bird-watching locations on the continent.

Following pages: A fishing boat pulls into harbor, Port Dover.

A congregation of gulls gathers on a sea wall,
Port Dover, Ontario.

Opposite page: It looks too cold for swimming:
Port Stanley Beach, Lake Erie.

Lake Ontario

Beauty, Silas thought, has a strange effect on people. "Makes them want to gush." Whether it takes the form of a fine concert, or a flash of feathers against the sun, or the falls of Niagara, beauty makes "people want to reach for words. But words always come up short, and the effect is to diminish what you've just felt. With some things it's best to look or listen and feel and think and keep your thoughts to yourself."

This is not, of course, something many can do, as you can judge for yourself if you stand by the railing beside the thundering falls and listen.

Louis Hennepin happened this way in 1678 and later wrote that he'd seen falls 600 feet high. People ever since have been exaggerating their claims about Niagara, exaggerations that are scarcely needed.

"Mostly," said Silas, "the exaggeration is in aid of making a profit." A spectacle of any kind, man-made or natural, seems to lure hucksters out of the woodwork. The bigger the spectacle, the more crowded the sideshow it invariably spawns, as a quick walk around the museums, souvenir stands, and gift shops of Niagara Falls confirms.

The falls have lured more than hustlers as some of these so-called museums reveal. Inside you see photographs of people who have walked tight-ropes stretched across Niagara's gaping maw, others who have leapt into its frothing pool, and still others who have gone over in barrels. Some have even lived to tell the tale.

We, on the other hand, lined up with dozens of others to don slickers and ride in a *Maid of the Mist* to the foot of the falls. "Legend has it that an Indian maiden, in despair most likely, over the loss of a love, leapt into the river to her romantic death. Legend also has it," said Silas, "that a god of the falls saved her at the last minute.

Either way, you're supposed to be able to see her image in the mist."

We looked.

Early in the nineteenth century, England was involved in another of her wars—this time with Napoleon—and was having a tough time of it. She needed sailors, but a lot of her erstwhile sailors had jumped ship for higher-paying and safer work, aboard American merchant ships. Her Majesty's service, in typical British fashion, simply stopped American ships and conducted searches for errant navy men. The Americans were properly enraged.

This high-handedness, coupled with other injustices real and imagined, caused the Americans to declare war on their former rulers.

England was, of course, a long way off so the Americans decided to vent their spleen on her closest possession: Canada.

"Truth of it was," said Silas, "Canada was the real issue all along. Every time the Americans tried to expand their frontiers to the west, they were attacked and driven back by the Indians. Besides, the Americans thought it was kind of silly to have two countries on one continent when one would be so much, well, neater."

It had not escaped the Americans' attention that Britain was fully occupied elsewhere, and that their own population of seven and a half million compared, for military purposes, quite nicely with the half million residents to the north.

"So war it was, and one of the most decisive battles was fought right here."

We were standing on Queenston Heights, in the shadow of Brock's Monument. "Isaac Brock was one smart fellow." He had orchestrated the surprising capture of the fort on Mackinac Island, and he had personally bluffed

General William Hull out of his fort at Detroit, with never a shot or arrow fired.

"Hull was terrified of the Indians. So Brock sent him a note saying he didn't mind a fight, but there was no telling what his Indian followers would do, once they got over the palisades. But it's up to you, Bill. . . . The very next day Hull came out and handed over the keys to the fort."

The Niagara Frontier was the next obvious American target. After two humiliations at the hands of a supposedly pushover militia, they were ready for blood.

"Brock, here, made his only serious miscalculation of the war. He would have bet his wages the Americans would cross the lower river and try to take Fort George." Outnumbered, he had to wait and see. In mid-October, he saw the Americans massing on the opposite shore, but farther upriver across from Queenston. "It was so obvious—they were all right there on the riverbank—that he figured they were trying to dupe him. Wrong guess."

A few nights later, he heard gunfire on Queenston Heights. The Americans had taken a page out of the British book and attacked the frontier as the British had attacked Quebec—the hard and least likely way.

Brock sent word to Fort George. Then he took what men he had and led a charge up the heights, and was promptly shot and killed. But when the Americans heard the reinforcements coming, "they suddenly remembered their constitutional rights. When they'd signed up, the forms had said nothing about fighting on foreign soil. Their commander, Winfield Scott, standing on the shore and watching them paddling for home, had only one option: it was white and he waved it."

When it comes to shorelines, Lake Ontario is Erie's opposite. More than a quarter of Canada's population is crowded into the crescent-shaped northeast coast, the Golden Horseshoe. From Hamilton in the west, to Oshawa in the east, the coast is heavily industrialized. As the economy has benefited from the steel mills and auto plants, the lake has suffered.

The American shore, with the exception of Rochester, is largely rural and undeveloped. The same force—the Erie Canal—which created congestion along Erie's south shore, lured industry and commerce away from the south shore of the lake. After passing through Rochester, the Erie Canal leads south and east to the Hudson.

It was along this shore we travelled, past Oswego, once, thanks to Canada's lumber, a thriving mill town, and Sackets Harbor, where the first shots in the War of 1812 were fired, to Kingston.

"By the second half of the eighteenth century the Americans had had it up to here with the British. Their taxes had been raised. Royal officials were interfering with their legislatures. Their trade was being disrupted and duties were being slapped on all kinds of goods to pay the salaries of the local toadies.

"The colonists figured it was high time they ran their own show. Since Britain didn't much like that idea, it came down to war.

"While most were in favor of independence, there were a lot of people with very strong loyalties to the Crown, and they fought long and hard to help the British win. When it was over and lost, they were not the most popular people south of the border.

"The ones who weren't shot, or tarred and feathered, or run out of the country on a rail, quickly took their cue, and their leave. Some took the nearest and next boat to England, but most crossed the frontier and turned up at the nearest British fort. A good many of them came here, to the area at the eastern end of Lake Ontario, and along the north shore of the St. Lawrence."

In the late 1780s, this land wasn't much to look at. Although the French had originally built a fort where Kingston now stands, and a trading outpost was developed, much of the lakeshore and riverbank was bog and bush. It was title to this land that the newcomers received in return for their loyalty, and this land they started clearing, at a pace of two or three acres a year, to make way for cabins and crops.

It was the single most important influx of immigrants to Upper Canada because the values and ethics of these newcomers shaped the society that welcomed them.

"This," said Silas a few days later, as we passed Toronto on our way to Port Credit, "is all the fault of John Graves Simcoe. If it weren't for him, this would probably be no bigger than Owen Sound."

Late in the eighteenth century, the town of Newark was the capital of Upper Canada, but Upper Canada's first lieutenant-governor thought it was too vulnerable to attack by the Americans. He moved the capital to the far-distant village of York which, when the War of 1812 broke out, was invaded twice and almost burned to the ground.

York grew up to become Toronto, and Newark grew hardly at all to become Niagara-on-the-Lake. "Both of them, and most of the rest of Upper Canada, came to belong to the gentry and the gentry, with their strong merchant, British and Loyalist backgrounds, were not overly fond of the rabble. The rabble—the farmers and workers—were making a lot of rude noise about the need for more freedom, and better representation in matters governmental."

While life went gently on, some people chafed. No one was more vocal or voluble than William Lyon Mackenzie, who, unhappily for the Family Compact, had both a printing press and the intelligence to put it to good use.

Mackenzie succeeded, finally, in fomenting considerable disaffection. "The upshot of it was that Mackenzie and a group of disgruntled farmers met at a tavern, and settled on a march down Yonge Street to seize the city and set things to rights.

"What encouraged them along was the news that the garrison had headed off to Lower Canada to quell a rebellion there. Unfortunately, as they soon found out, there were more than enough soldiers, with guns, to send the pitchfork brigade back to their fields.

"Mackenzie made himself scarce. Under cover of darkness, and with no little help from sympathizers along the way, he finally fled to New York. He and some of his followers set up a provisional government. They made their headquarters on Navy Island, in the Niagara River, and waited for their chance to invade Canada. But with the exception of a couple of skirmishes, the Rebellion of 1837 was over.

"The thing was," said Silas, "though he was defeated, he never gave up. After spending a decade in the United States, he was pardoned. He promptly came home and got himself elected to the legislative assembly. To the end of his days, on the floor of the House, in public speeches, or in the pages of his newspaper, he just went on speaking his mind. Consequences be damned.

"Altogether," said Silas, "my kind of man."

The locks in the Welland Canal lower shipping
more than 300 feet on the way from Lake Erie to
Lake Ontario.

Opposite page: A ship goes down—as they release
water from the lock—in the Welland Canal.

Following pages: Sailboats moored beside
Bluffer's Park, near Toronto, Ontario.

The Welland Canal is not much wider than some of the traffic it carries.

Opposite page: A lighthouse overlooks the Bay of Quinte, on Lake Ontario's north shore.

Prince Edward County keeps alive the traditions of the Loyalists who came to Canada after U.S. independence.

The Loyalists settled along Lake Ontario's north shore, and prospered. Their descendents don costumes for tourists in this pioneer village.

Following pages: Some of nature's works cannot be adequately described in words—the falls at Niagara among them.

Winter ice makes Niagara Falls almost as
spectacular as the sunshine does in summer.

You're supposed to be able to see an Indian maiden in the spray thrown up by the Falls.

Following pages: The Glenora Ferry makes its way across the Bay of Quinte.

Boats moored to a quay in winter: Toronto, Ontario.

Toronto's CN Tower, the world's tallest free-standing structure, dominates the distant skyline.

Sport fishermen try their luck below the sand dunes, Bay of Quinte.

Following pages: Gulls stand guard on wooden railings beside the Welland Canal.

A fisherman's nets capture the dying sun in the Bay of Quinte.

An old bridge casts its shadow in the water, in Rochester, New York.

Niagara Falls generates a million tourist photographs—and hydro-electric power, which these lines then carry away.

Old Fort Henry guards the promontory which overlooks Kingston, Ontario.

Postscript

Silas John is long in his grave, but of him and our trip a host of images refuses to fade.

One dazzling, cloudless, pines-framed day, we dove from *Persephone*'s deck into the waters of Georgian Bay, waters so clear you'd swear you could hold your nose and touch the gargantuan boulders below. "Go ahead," he said, "and give it a try." Try as I did, those boulders which looked so close were thirty feet or more beyond my reach.

Earlier that morning I had rowed *Zeus*, the dinghy, around a shoulder of granite into an adjacent bay. At the far end, there was a kind of marsh where Silas guessed I would find our supper finning around. I could see that pike and many of his like, in those diaphanous waters, long before I hauled him over the dinghy's gunwale.

And, finally, this: many more times than once Silas dipped his knobby-knuckled hands into the reflection of his grinning face and drank the water.

These three images, perhaps more than any others, sum up what was finest about these lakes of ours when I was first introduced to them.

Our collective and corporate lust for profit has changed all that.

Poisons whose names we cannot pronounce have been poured, and are being poured daily, in amounts and combinations that may only be described as criminal, into the waters which we drink.

Our industries lack the moral sense to stop this wanton destruction of our most precious resource, and our governments lack the political will to force them to do so.

Our children will wonder why.

Silas was prodded to anger twice on our voyage: once by the sight and smell of the south coast of Lake Michigan and again by the eye-stinging Chemical Valley of the St. Clair.

He said, then, "it's more than a shame."

Three decades later, it still is.